ANIMAL BESTS

MARINE SUPERSTARS

Thanks to the creative team:
Senior Editor: Alice Peebles
Fact checking: Kate Mitchell
Design: www.collaborate.agency

Hungry Tomato™
A division of Lerner Publishing Group, Inc.
241 First Avenue North
Minneapolis, MN 55401 USA

For reading levels and more information, look up
this title at www.lernerbooks.com.

Main body text set in Mate Regular 10/12.

Library of Congress Cataloging-in-Publication Data

The Cataloging-in-Publication Data for *Marine
Superstars* is on file at the Library of Congress.
ISBN 978-1-5124-0625-2 (lib. bdg.)
ISBN 978-1-5124-1168-3 (pbk.)
ISBN 978-1-5124-0919-2 (EB pdf)

Manufactured in the United States of America
1-39298-21135-3/24/2016

ANIMAL BESTS

MARINE SUPERSTARS

BY JOHN FARNDON
ILLUSTRATED BY CRISTINA PORTOLANO

HUNGRY TOMATO.

CUTTLEFISH DON'T LOOK
LIKE MUCH MORE THAN
STRETCHED-OUT OCTOPUSES,
BUT THEY HAVE SOME
PRETTY SPECIAL SKILLS!

CONTENTS

ANIMALS IN THE SEA

Nearly all animals are very good at what they were born to do—far better than humans. And they have special skills and characteristics that help them to survive. This book introduces you to some of the cleverest and best adapted sea creatures.

Here's a taste of how amazing sea creatures are, before we even get on to the really clever stuff . . .

SPRINTERS

The fastest creature in the sea is the black marlin (left). A marlin can shoot through the water at 80 miles per hour (130 kilometers per hour). Scientists gauge this by how quickly it unravels a fishing line. It also travels extraordinary distances. One that was tagged in California was later found 10,000 miles (16,000 km) away in New Zealand.

HIGH JUMP

Salmon (below) spend most of their lives in the sea, but they save their best jumping for when they head upriver to breed. Salmon can leap up waterfalls 12 feet (3.65 meters) high—that's about six times their own length.

LONG JUMP

Flying fish (right) can leap out of the water and glide through the air for more than 160 feet (50 m). Occasionally, they travel 1,300 feet (400 m). It is thought they do this to escape their many predators. Their large, winglike fins get them airborne, and they are carried along by winds and air currents.

ALL-ROUNDER

Dolphins are the freestyle champions of the animal world. They can leap 20 feet (6 m) out of the water and swim 33 miles per hour (54 km/h). They can also do all kinds of acrobatic twists and turns, and balance a ball on their nose while swimming backward. And they do it on porpoise . . .

POWERHOUSES

The strongest creature in the sea is the blue whale (right), which can shift its huge weight (usually around 110 tons (100 tonnes)) along at over 20 miles per hour (30 km/h). It can keep this up for long distances.

UNDERSEA BRAINBOXES

They may look really odd with their eight tentacles, large suckers, and boggly eyes, but octopuses may be the brainiest sea creatures. They are the cleverest of invertebrates (animals without backbones). They alone can learn new tasks and solve problems.

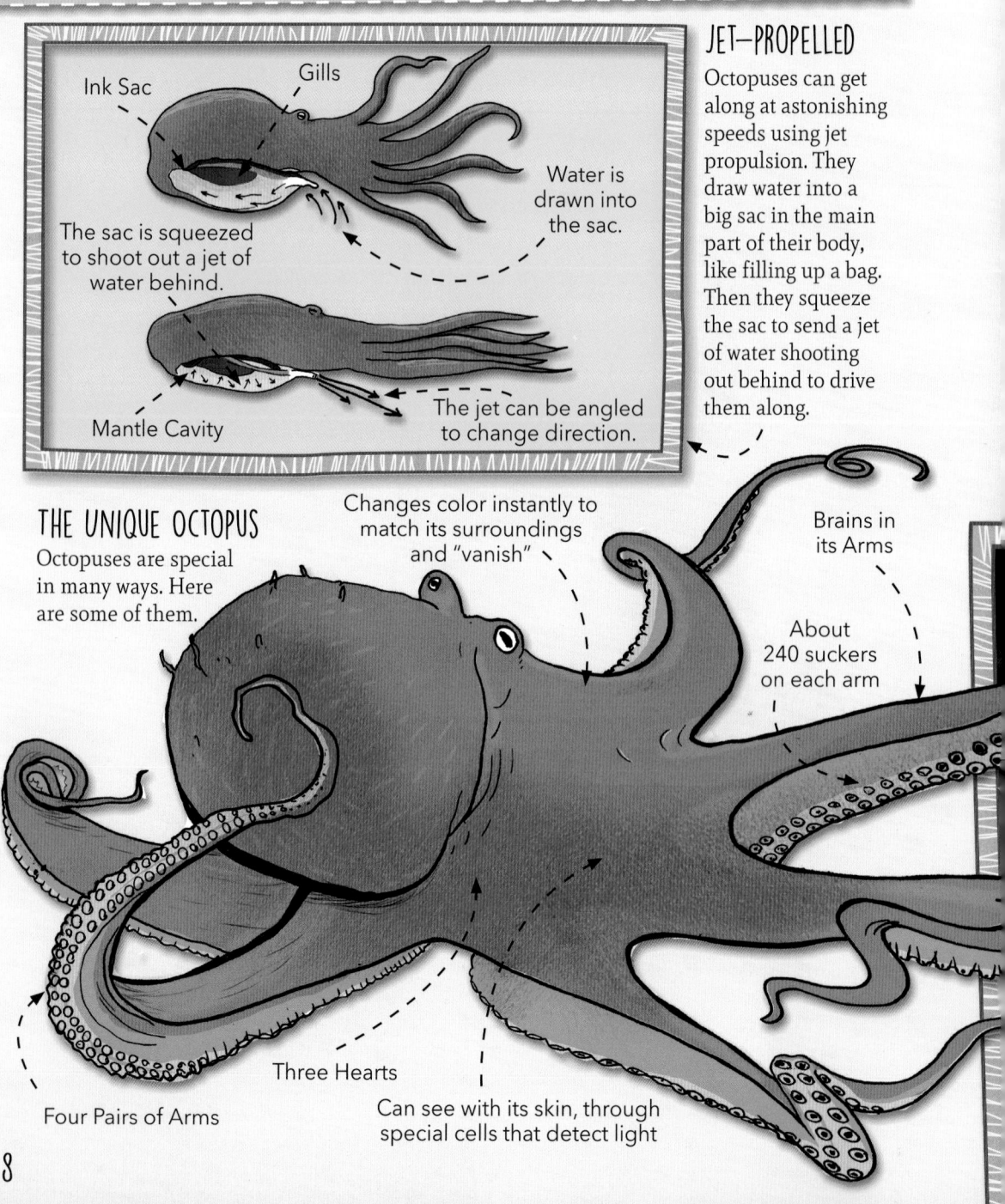

Ink Sac

Gills

Water is drawn into the sac.

The sac is squeezed to shoot out a jet of water behind.

Mantle Cavity

The jet can be angled to change direction.

JET–PROPELLED

Octopuses can get along at astonishing speeds using jet propulsion. They draw water into a big sac in the main part of their body, like filling up a bag. Then they squeeze the sac to send a jet of water shooting out behind to drive them along.

THE UNIQUE OCTOPUS

Octopuses are special in many ways. Here are some of them.

Changes color instantly to match its surroundings and "vanish"

Brains in its Arms

About 240 suckers on each arm

Four Pairs of Arms

Three Hearts

Can see with its skin, through special cells that detect light

GET INTO THAT

Faced with some food inside a closed glass jar, an octopus can work out that to get at the food, it must unscrew the lid. With its arm-like tentacles, it can open the jar in seconds—a feat that would be too hard for any other animal, except humans with their clever hands.

GET OUT OF THAT!

In some experiments, scientists put an octopus inside a glass jar and screwed on the lid. Amazingly, the octopus realized that to escape it must unscrew the lid from underneath. Using the suckers on its tentacles, it gripped the flat of the lid to turn it and open the jar.

TOOL USERS

Octopuses were the first invertebrates ever seen to use tools—something many animal experts see as a sign of intelligence. Some pick up empty coconut shells and carry them like mobile homes, as protection against predators. They may also use rocks or shells in the same way. Some even curl up inside a shelter, such as an old jar.

SLICK COMMUNICATORS

Whales are perhaps the most amazing communicators in the world. In good conditions, blue whales can talk to each other over a distance of 1,000 miles (1,600 km), and they make the deepest sounds of any animal. A whale's brain might have only two-thirds as many cells as a human's, but it's six times bigger!

ANNUAL MIGRATION OF THE BLUE WHALE

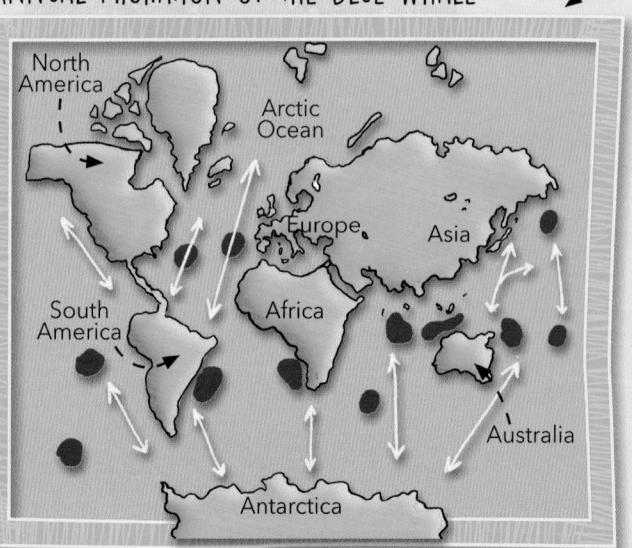

North America
Arctic Ocean
Europe
Asia
South America
Africa
Australia
Antarctica

■ = Winter Breeding Area   □ = Migration Paths

WHALE JOURNEYS

Whales are mighty travelers. In summer they swim far into icy polar waters to feed on the wealth of tiny sea creatures there. In winter they return to the tropics to breed and give birth. Some grey whales migrate 10,000–12,400 miles (16,000–20,000 km) every year. One female grey made a single round-trip of 14,000 miles (22,500 km)!

THANK YOU!

Whales are capable of complex emotions and interactions. Sadly, it has become common for whales to get caught up in fishing nets. When that happens, they soon die. Once, when a humpback was tangled in nets, fishermen worked to free it—and when they succeeded, the whale seemed to swim around joyfully as if to say thank you.

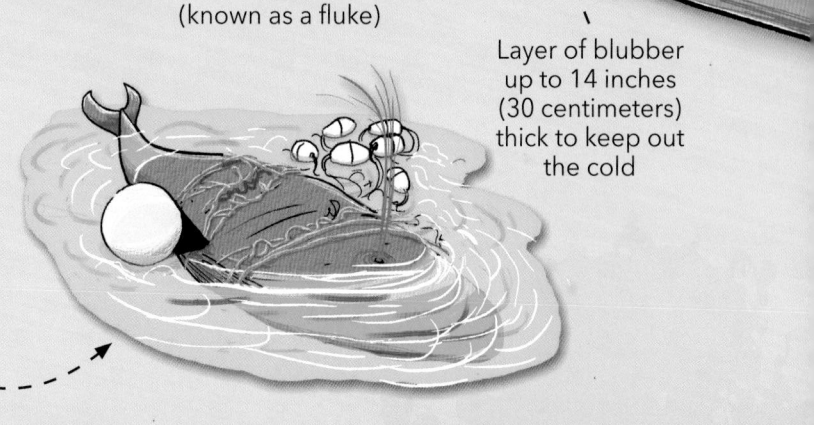

Small Dorsal Fin

Tail Fin (known as a fluke)

Layer of blubber up to 14 inches (30 centimeters) thick to keep out the cold

WHALE TALK

To human ears, humpback whale sounds seem like squeaks and grunts. But to another humpback, that sound is music. Male humpbacks have the most complex, eerie, and beautiful songs of any animal. They sing mainly when they're in warm water. When they do, they hang in the water nose down. No one knows why they sing.

HOW WHALES MAKE NOISE

Blue whales are really, really loud. Their call can reach up to 188 decibels—much, much louder than a jet plane—and can be heard hundreds of miles away. A sperm whale (right) makes the sound by taking air in through its nasal passages when it goes up for air—then forcing it out through the flaps on its nose called "monkey lips."

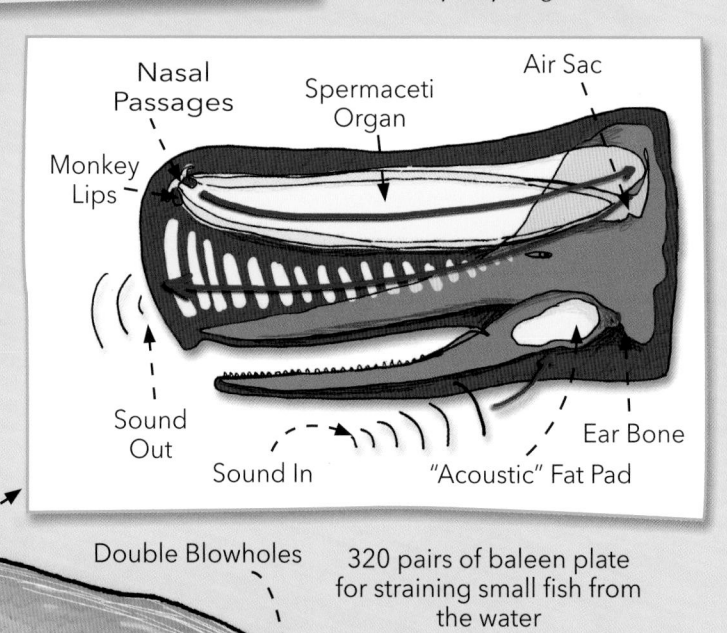

Nasal Passages
Monkey Lips
Spermaceti Organ
Air Sac
Sound Out
Sound In
"Acoustic" Fat Pad
Ear Bone

Double Blowholes

320 pairs of baleen plate for straining small fish from the water

A whale can take in 11,000 pounds (5,000 kilograms) of water and plankton in each gulp

Flipper up to 8 feet (2.5 m) long

Size Comparison

BIG BLUE

The blue whale is the biggest creature ever. Its tongue weighs as much as an elephant and you could crawl through the valves in its heart. The largest specimen ever seen was some 100 feet (30 m) long and weighed 220 tons (200 tonnes).

DETECTOR POWER

The sonar systems used by submarines to detect things in the water may seem like clever human technology beyond any animal. But dolphins have been using their own sonar system, known as echolocation, for millions of years. It's so acute that they can tell the difference between a tiny seed and a metal pellet 50 feet (16 m) away underwater.

CARING DOLPHINS

When hunting, dolphins work together and share tasks—sometimes not just with other dolphins. In west Africa, they drive shoals of fish toward nets to trap them. The fishermen wait for the dolphins to eat, then haul in the catch. Dolphins also protect human swimmers from sharks! Dolphins in Australia are known to come into shore to play with children.

FINNY FUN

Playing is often thought to be a sign of intelligence. If so, dolphins are super clever. Few animals seem to enjoy playing as much as dolphins. People now realize it's cruel to keep them in tanks and teach them tricks. But dolphins seem to love games with balls, playing catch with a fish, or even playing tag. They make sounds like laughter when they do!

BOW-RIDING

Dolphins seem fascinated by ships. They often ride the bow wave sent up from the front of a ship, like surfers riding a wave. This is called bow-riding, and dolphins have been doing it ever since ships have existed. No one knows why. Some say they are hitching a ride. Some say they are showing off. But they may just be doing it for fun.

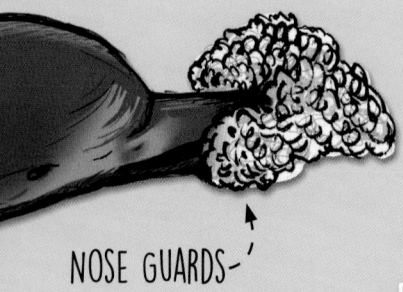

NOSE GUARDS

A dolphin's nose is soft and easily damaged, so some Pacific Bottlenose dolphins have learned to pick up a sponge to protect it when they're foraging among sharp rocks. Mother dolphins teach this trick to younger dolphins, or to newcomers to an area.

CLICKETY CLICK

To locate things underwater, a dolphin sends out a series of clicks and squeaks from its nose—some at much too high a pitch for us to hear. When the sound hits something, it bounces back as an echo. From the way the sound echoes back, the dolphin can tell just where the object is. This is echolocation.

SUPER—JUMP

Dolphins can jump clean out of the water, up to 20 feet (6 m) in the air. Scientists have tried to guess why they do these amazing leaps. Some think it might be to get a better view. Others think they could be shaking off parasites. But as with bow-riding, they could just be having a whale of a time . . .

LEARNING TOGETHER

A few clever animals can learn new things. But dolphins especially pass on what they know and learn from each other. Kelly, a dolphin in a US research center, was trained to keep her tank clean with the reward of a fish for every bit of litter she found. When Kelly found some paper, she tore it into pieces and hid them under a stone, so she could claim a fish for every piece—and she taught her daughter to do the same!

SUPER SENSES

Catfish are one of the most extraordinary and underrated animal groups in the sea. They live almost everywhere in the world. That's partly because they have super senses and special abilities that enable them to survive in all kinds of places, including murky, muddy ponds and ice-covered pools, which would be uninhabitable for most fish.

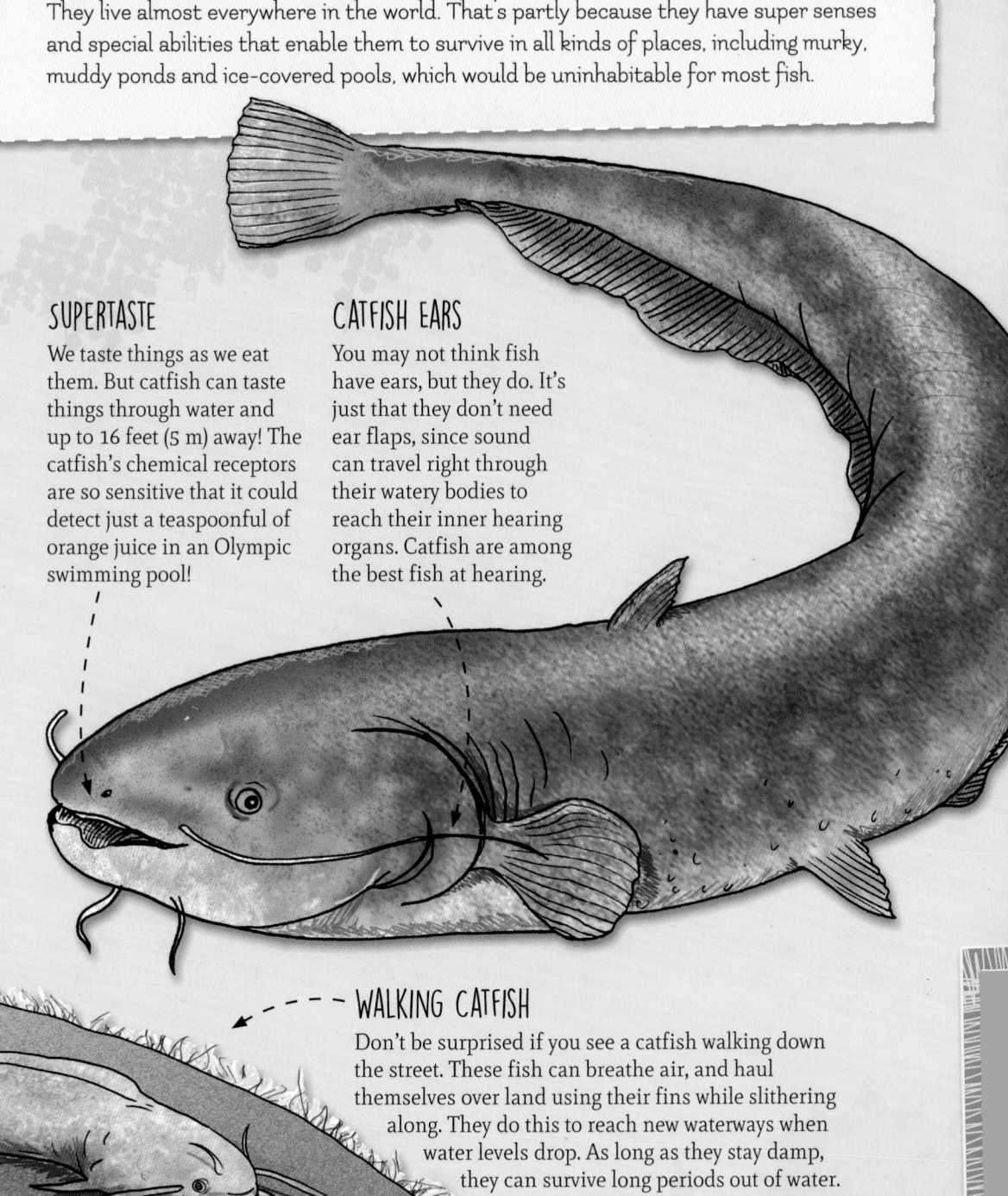

SUPERTASTE

We taste things as we eat them. But catfish can taste things through water and up to 16 feet (5 m) away! The catfish's chemical receptors are so sensitive that it could detect just a teaspoonful of orange juice in an Olympic swimming pool!

CATFISH EARS

You may not think fish have ears, but they do. It's just that they don't need ear flaps, since sound can travel right through their watery bodies to reach their inner hearing organs. Catfish are among the best fish at hearing.

WALKING CATFISH

Don't be surprised if you see a catfish walking down the street. These fish can breathe air, and haul themselves over land using their fins while slithering along. They do this to reach new waterways when water levels drop. As long as they stay damp, they can survive long periods out of water. Some catfish can even climb walls!

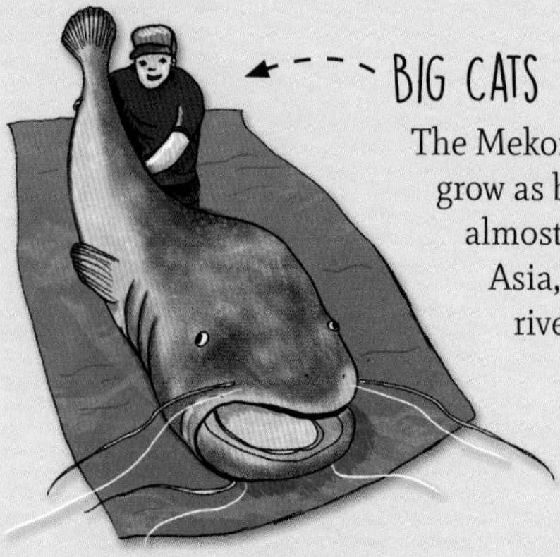

BIG CATS

The Mekong Giant Catfish is the world's biggest freshwater fish. It can grow as big as a tiger, nearly 10 feet (3 m) long, and tip the scales at almost 650 pounds (300 kg). It lives in the Mekong River in Southeast Asia, but is now very rare because of environmental damage to the river, and because too many fishermen have caught it.

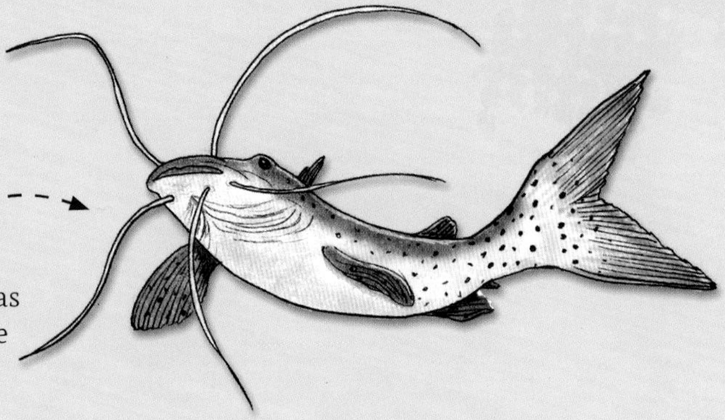

WHY DO CATFISH HAVE WHISKERS?

Catfish get their name from their extraordinary catlike whiskers, known as barbels. Barbels help to give catfish one of their super senses: taste. Catfish are like swimming tongues, with taste buds all over their body—175,000 in all. But these are most concentrated on their barbels and in their gills.

HYPERTASTE

Catfish have a pretty exceptional sense of taste, perfect for living in murky environments where you can't see what you're eating. But a catfish's taste power is nothing compared to the American eel's. This eel could taste seven cartons of orange juice poured into the whole of Scotland's biggest lake, Loch Ness.

SILENT MAJORITY

Bristlemouth fish may well be the most numerous animals in the world. But they are so elusive that they are hard to count. They live deep in the ocean—more than 1,000 feet (330 m) down—and like many deep-sea fish have very acute senses, so that they can detect and avoid the fine nets scientists use to sample the depths.

SMART SURVIVORS

For divers, a tropical coral reef is an underwater paradise, teeming with life. But the creatures that live there have a constant battle for survival. It is a magnet for predators, such as barracuda, moray eels, and groupers. Reef inhabitants, such as the parrotfish, have developed clever strategies to avoid becoming dinner.

COLOR PALETTE

Parrotfish change their colorful looks all the time. Some can change color to mimic other fish and fool predators. But they also change color throughout their lives. Baby parrotfish typically start life a dull red or brown, but as they mature they turn vivid shades of green and blue, with pink and yellow patches. Most also change their sex, too, starting life as female and becoming male later on.

CHOPPERS!

When a parrotfish opens its mouth, you can see it has the toothiest grin of any fish. The teeth look cartoon-like, but they're real and necessary. With those tough teeth, parrotfish can bite off chunks of bony coral and grind it down to get at the green algae inside that they love.

LOOK AT HOW BIG I AM! - - - - - -

The pufferfish is rather slow, and could never race away from a predator to save its life. Instead, it fills its stomach with water so that it blows up like a soccer ball to two or three times its size. This not only makes it more scary. It makes it too much of a mouthful, especially with its prickly, sometimes poisonous spikes.

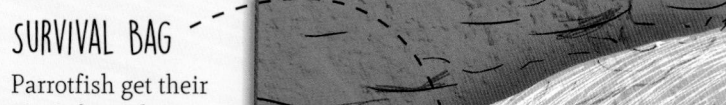

FISH BEACH

Parrotfish can't digest the coral they grind down for the algae, so they excrete it as fine white sand. That white sand forms the beautiful white tropical beaches where people on vacation love to visit. Maybe they wouldn't like the beaches so much if they knew they were parrotfish poo!

SURVIVAL BAG

Parrotfish get their name from their gorgeous parrot-like colors and strange beak-like mouths. When they go to sleep at night, they blow up a ball of mucus (saliva) to make their own protective sleeping bag. The bag hides their scent from hunting eels. It also gives them a millisecond's warning if an eel is getting close.

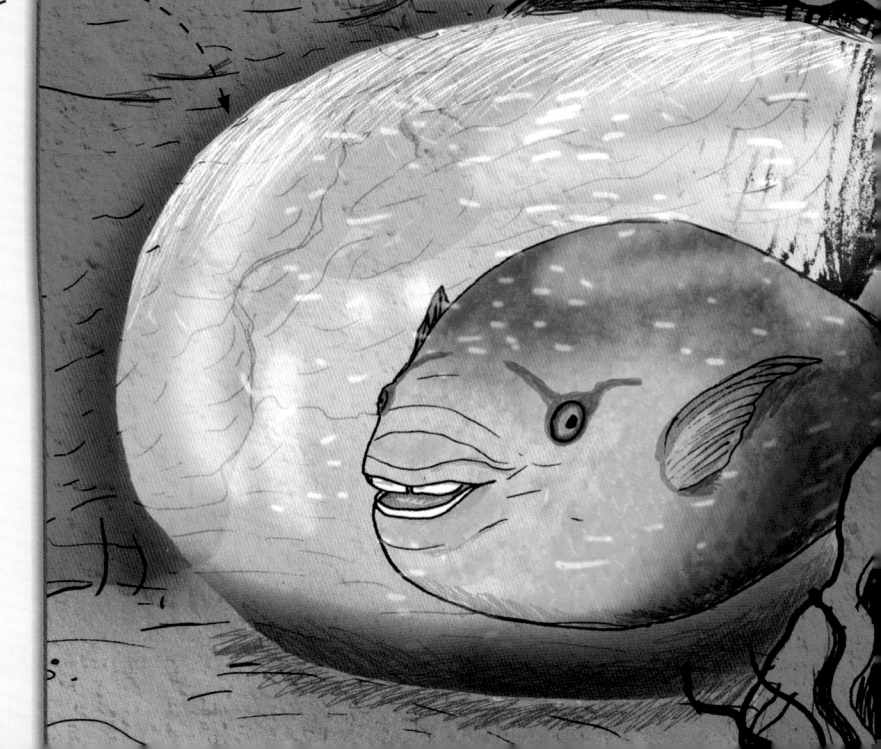

ESCAPE ARTISTS

The best way for sea creatures to avoid being eaten by predators is to avoid being seen. Jellyfish are hard to see when they are transparent. Many fish are covered in shiny scales that give off confusing reflections. Others have developed very neat kinds of camouflage.

WEEDY DRAGON

The aptly named leafy seadragon lives off the south coast of Australia. It is a very slow swimmer, and is very unlikely to outrun a predator. But its body is covered in leaflike fronds that look so much like seaweed it is very hard to spot. Yet leafy seadragons are now quite rare, partly because their habitat has been damaged by pollution, and partly because they are caught to use in alternative medicine.

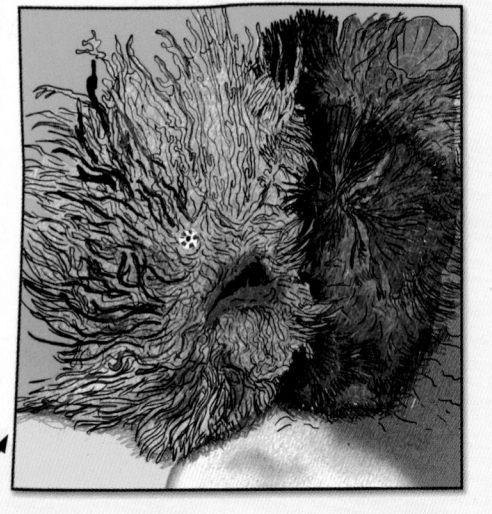

HIDDEN ANGLER

Beautiful anglerfish of the rivers and sea are popular for aquariums because of their graceful shapes and shimmering colors. But tasselled anglerfish look very different—if you can see them at all. They are not colorful, but are covered in waving fronds that give them a perfect seaweed disguise.

MOVING HOUSE

Unlike most crabs, the hermit crab has no flat, hard shell. Instead, it lives inside the discarded shell of another creature, such as a whelk. The hermit crab is shaped like a snail so that it slips easily inside a shell. The shell is both its mobile home and a suit of armor. As the crab grows, it simply throws away its shell and moves into a bigger one.

Hermit Crab (without shell)

Hermit Crab (with shell)

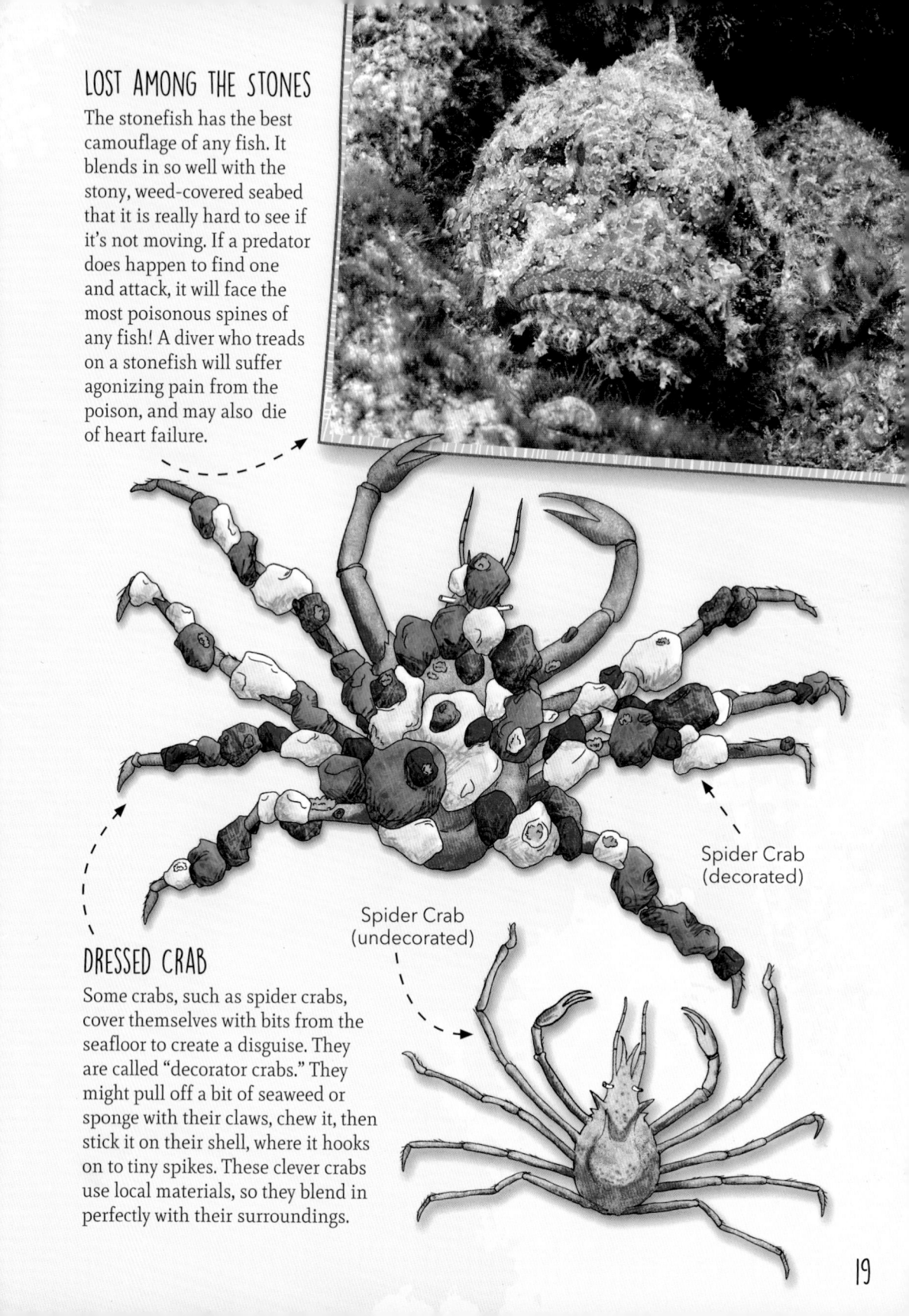

LOST AMONG THE STONES

The stonefish has the best camouflage of any fish. It blends in so well with the stony, weed-covered seabed that it is really hard to see if it's not moving. If a predator does happen to find one and attack, it will face the most poisonous spines of any fish! A diver who treads on a stonefish will suffer agonizing pain from the poison, and may also die of heart failure.

Spider Crab
(decorated)

Spider Crab
(undecorated)

DRESSED CRAB

Some crabs, such as spider crabs, cover themselves with bits from the seafloor to create a disguise. They are called "decorator crabs." They might pull off a bit of seaweed or sponge with their claws, chew it, then stick it on their shell, where it hooks on to tiny spikes. These clever crabs use local materials, so they blend in perfectly with their surroundings.

19

DECOY DIVAS AND DEEP CUNNING

Some sea creatures use all kinds of trickery to catch their prey—or make a crafty getaway. Cuttlefish throw out a smokescreen of ink to hide behind. Scorpionfish and frogfish have bait attached to their fins to draw in prey. And sharks play dead!

ANGLERFISH

In the depths of the ocean, it is so dark that even fish can't see much. That's why the bright light hung out by the anglerfish, like the bait on an angler's fishing rod, makes a very good lure. The light, dangling in front of the anglerfish, comes from luminescent (light-giving) chemicals that glow naturally. Little fish that are drawn to the light will swim straight into the anglerfish's mouth!

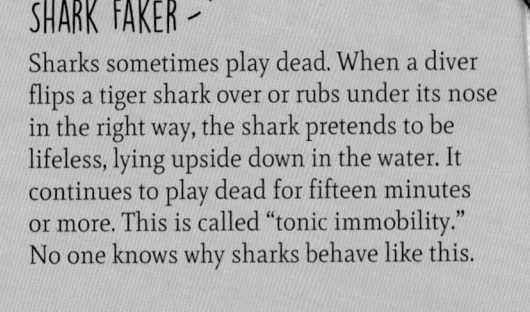

SHARK FAKER

Sharks sometimes play dead. When a diver flips a tiger shark over or rubs under its nose in the right way, the shark pretends to be lifeless, lying upside down in the water. It continues to play dead for fifteen minutes or more. This is called "tonic immobility." No one knows why sharks behave like this.

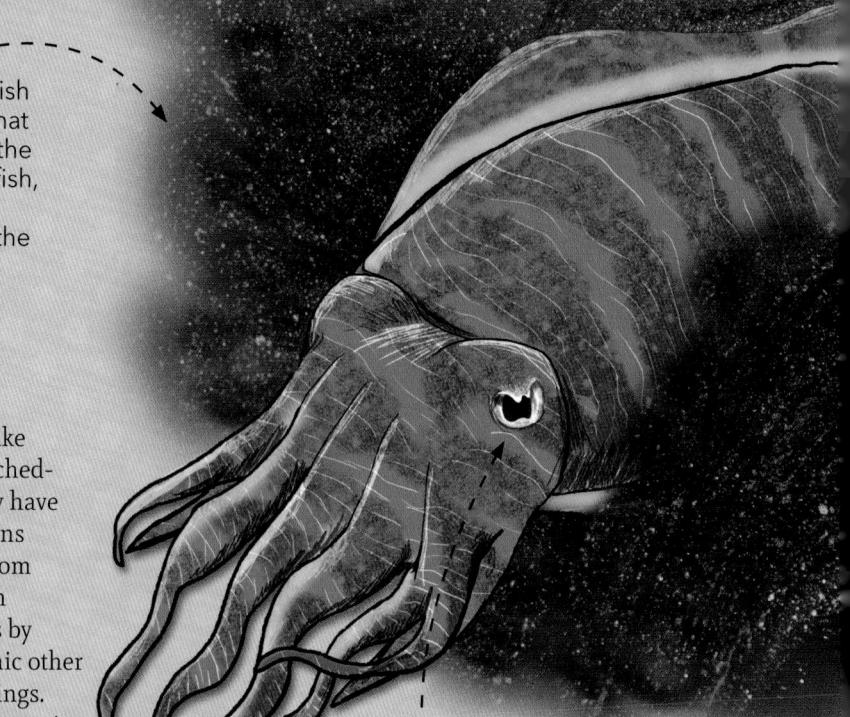

Sometimes cuttlefish make ink clouds that look so much like the shadow of a cuttlefish, that predators mistakenly attack the clouds instead!

INKY ESCAPE

Cuttlefish don't look like much more than stretched-out octopuses. Yet they have one of the biggest brains of any invertebrate. From a young age, they learn to disguise themselves by changing color to mimic other fish or their surroundings. And if threatened, they squirt out a cloud of black ink to hide their escape.

CUTTLEFISH EYES

One of the cuttlefish's super powers is its eyesight. If you wear polarized sunglasses on a sunny day, you can see more clearly because the glasses cut out reflections that create a glare on shiny surfaces. A cuttlefish's eyes can see how light is polarized, whatever the angle. They not only see very clearly through water, but also adjust their body color so precisely they become almost invisible.

ARTY FISH

Writers have used cuttlefish ink since the times of ancient Greece. This brown ink was named *sepia* after a kind of cuttlefish found there. Most famously, the artist Leonardo da Vinci (1452–1519) used sepia in many of his sketches and notes, including his sketch of the Vitruvian man. This showed the ideal geometric relationship between parts of the human body.

KILLERS OF THE DEEP

Great white sharks are the ocean's deadliest hunters. They have super strong, sleek bodies and a gaping mouth full of sharp, hard-biting teeth. And they have remarkable senses. They can sense a single drop of blood in the water from hundreds of feet away. They can even sense the faint electrical charges made by a victim's heart.

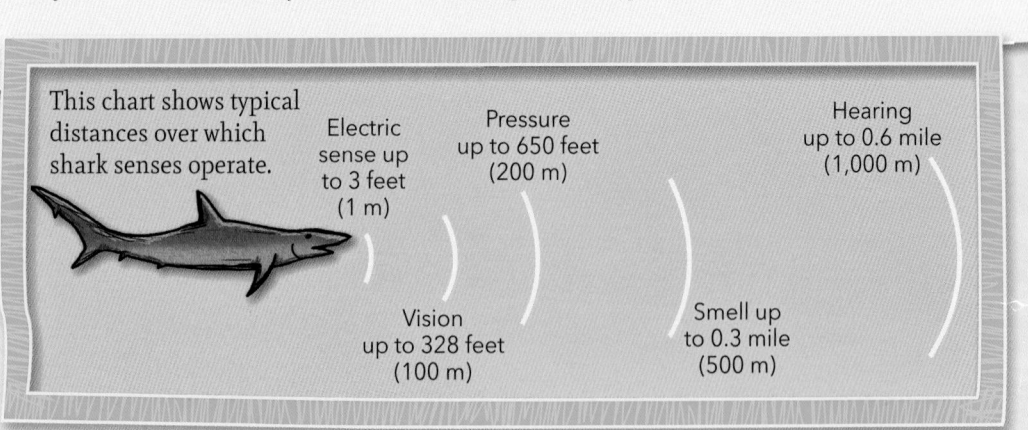

This chart shows typical distances over which shark senses operate.

Electric sense up to 3 feet (1 m)

Pressure up to 650 feet (200 m)

Hearing up to 0.6 mile (1,000 m)

Vision up to 328 feet (100 m)

Smell up to 0.3 mile (500 m)

NO HIDING

A shark on the lookout for prey uses different senses at different distances. A shark can hear sounds through the water from far away, and pick up distant faint scents so acutely that it can pinpoint the scents' locations. A shark can even detect the electric current of a heartbeat with small pores in its snout.

KILLING VIEW

Sharks can raise their heads far out of the water. It's thought they are getting a better view of their prey before going in for the kill, and the activity is called spy-hopping.

SHARK CAGE

In some parts of the world, thrill seekers in scuba-diving gear descend into the water inside tough steel cages to see sharks up close. Sharks hurl themselves at the cages to get at the divers, or grab the bars with a crushing bite. In theory, the cage will protect the divers, but there have been accidents.

NO ESCAPE

Sometimes, great white sharks can jump 6 feet (2 m) or more out of the water as they pounce on their prey. Even agile swimmers, such as seals, stand little chance of escaping.

SNACKING ON PENGUINS

When basking on the Antarctic ice, leopard seals look quite cute. But in the water, they are deadly hunters. A big leopard seal is the size of a leopard on land, and has teeth just as sharp. Penguins will not last long if they stray off the ice when a leopard seal is lurking in the water. It will eat twelve or more penguins a day.

GOT YOU!

After a great white shark has found its prey, it takes its time to go in for the kill. It hunts mainly in the early morning or evening, when most of the light bounces off the sea surface. Then the shark is barely visible as it slides along just behind and beneath its prey. At the right moment, the shark shoots up and lunges, inflicting terrible damage with its mighty bite.

MAKING ALLIES

Many sea creatures have found they survive better by working with other species. This is called symbiosis. Sometimes it seems an unlikely partnership. Cleaner shrimp feed right inside the mouth of the electric eel, which could easily swallow them for dinner. The eel lets them do this because they eat parasites that might infect its mouth.

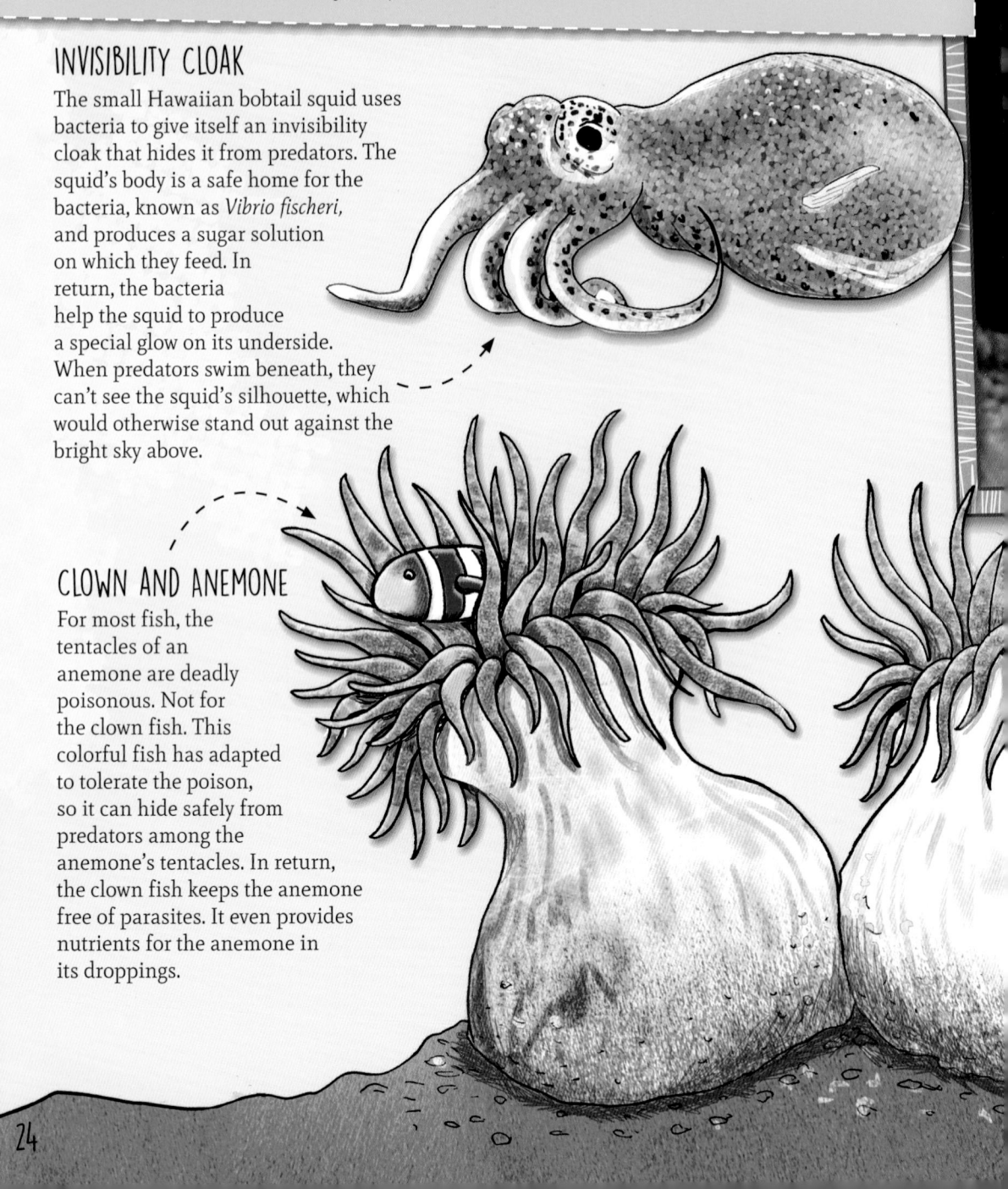

INVISIBILITY CLOAK

The small Hawaiian bobtail squid uses bacteria to give itself an invisibility cloak that hides it from predators. The squid's body is a safe home for the bacteria, known as *Vibrio fischeri,* and produces a sugar solution on which they feed. In return, the bacteria help the squid to produce a special glow on its underside. When predators swim beneath, they can't see the squid's silhouette, which would otherwise stand out against the bright sky above.

CLOWN AND ANEMONE

For most fish, the tentacles of an anemone are deadly poisonous. Not for the clown fish. This colorful fish has adapted to tolerate the poison, so it can hide safely from predators among the anemone's tentacles. In return, the clown fish keeps the anemone free of parasites. It even provides nutrients for the anemone in its droppings.

MAKEOVER ANYONE?

How do you keep clean and free from parasites if you're a reef fish? The answer is, you go to a wrasse cleaning station. Here, tiny fish called cleaner wrasse do a little dance to calm you down and get you ready. Then they set to work, nibbling away at your open mouth, your fins, and even inside your gills, to clean away parasites and other debris.

HOT WORMS

The Pompeii worm lives deep down on the seafloor in places called *hydrothermal vents*. Here, volcanic gases bubble up, heating the water almost to boiling point. Yet, strangely, the worms can survive. It's thought they tolerate the heat because they are protected by a thick coat of heat-tolerant bacteria. The bacteria, in turn, feed on a mucus secreted by the worm.

DO YOU WANT A FIGHT?

Boxer crabs really take advantage of their stinging anemone friends. They don't hide among their tentacles as clown fish do. Boxer crabs actually pick up the anemones with their pincers and wear them like boxing gloves. Any predator that comes their way will get a faceful of stinging tentacles.

25

TOOL USERS

The sea otter is one of the cutest-looking creatures in the sea. It is a mammal related to weasels, yet it spends most of its time in the sea. It has webbed feet, very, very thick fur to keep it dry and warm, and nostrils and ears that close in the water. And it's one of the few creatures, apart from humans and apes, that regularly use tools.

BEDTIME

After dinner, otters lie down and float off into dreamland. You can often see groups of otters having a nap together like this. But the otters don't want to drift out to sea while they're sleeping. So they wrap themselves in seaweed to create a weedy blanket that anchors them in place.

CLAM SMASHING

Otters like to eat clams. But clams have super-tough shells. So otters have learned to lie on their backs in the water with a big stone on their tummy. Then they grab the clam in their front paws and smash it on the stone again and again until it cracks open.

KEYSTONE SPECIES

Otters are quite few in number. There are probably less than 100,000 worldwide, and just 3,000 or so in California. Yet they are what is called a keystone species—they play a key role in the environment. Without sea otters, the creatures they feed on, such as sea urchins (right), would multiply. The urchins would then devour the forests of seaweed kelp that not only provide vital food and cover for other animals, but also help to control carbon dioxide levels in the air, which is damaging the world's climate.

WHO EATS WHO IN THE KELP FOREST

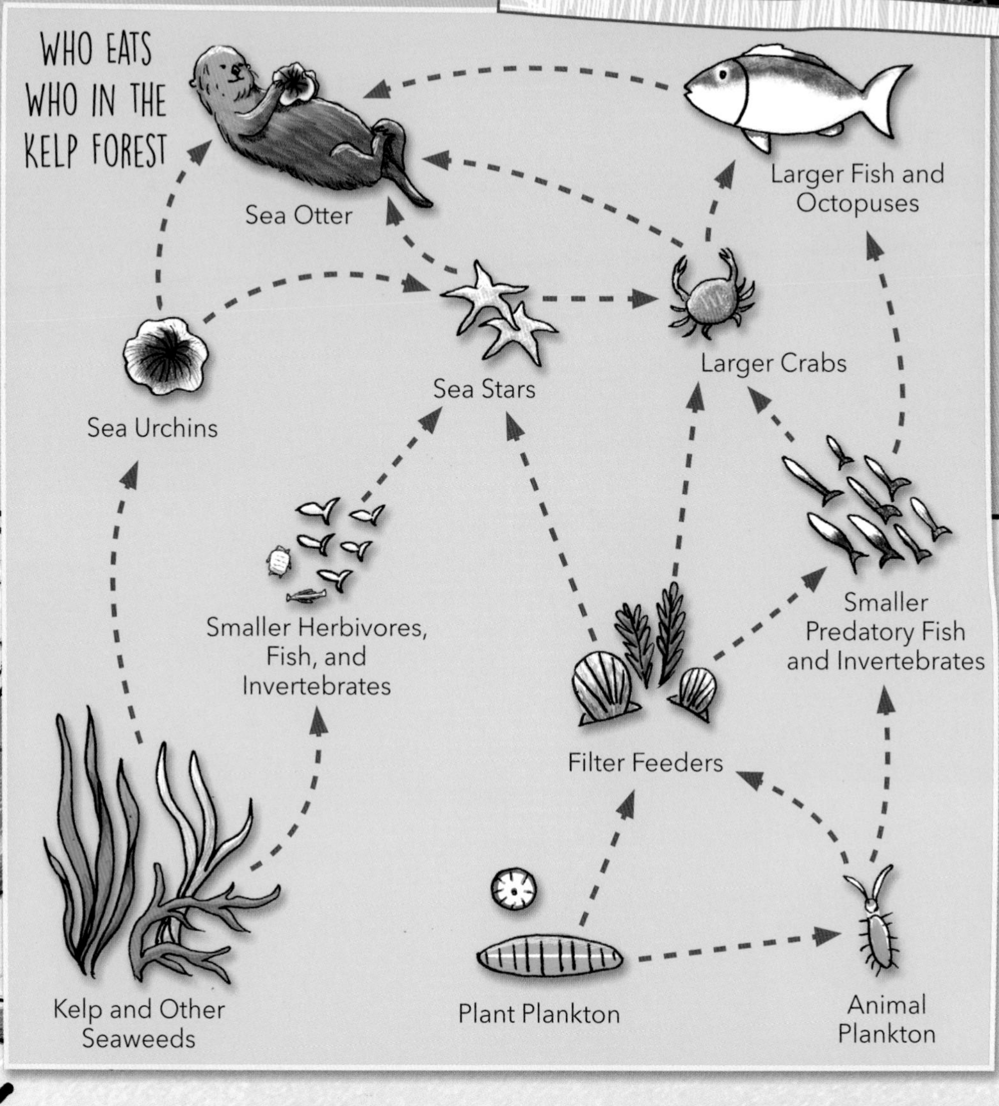

Sea Otter

Larger Fish and Octopuses

Sea Urchins

Sea Stars

Larger Crabs

Smaller Herbivores, Fish, and Invertebrates

Smaller Predatory Fish and Invertebrates

Filter Feeders

Kelp and Other Seaweeds

Plant Plankton

Animal Plankton

THE BEST OF THE BEST

OCTOPUSES
SPECIES: Close to 300
LIVE IN: Many ocean habitats, including coral reefs and the ocean floor
EAT: Crabs, worms, and small shellfish
KIND: Cephalopod mollusc

Octopuses have a beak, three hearts, and eight tentacles. They have no skeleton, so they can squeeze through very tight spaces.

WHALES
SPECIES: 85
LIVE IN: Near the surface, migrating from polar to warmer waters in summer
EAT: Baleen whales strain plankton and toothed whales hunt fish and octopuses
KIND: Cetacean mammal

Whales are mammals that breathe air. So they have to come up to the surface several times an hour, breathing through a blowhole on top of their head.

DOLPHINS
SPECIES: Close to 40
LIVE IN: Warm water in all oceans, but the killer whale prefers cooler water
EAT: Fish, such as herring, cod, or mackerel; killer whales hunt seals
KIND: Cetacean mammal

Dolphins are related to whales, and include the misleadingly named killer whale, as well as dolphins that live in rivers. They are also related to hippos.

CATFISH
SPECIES: 3,000–4,500
LIVE IN: Water everywhere except Antarctica
EAT: Other fish, invertebrates, aquatic plants, and fish eggs; as bottom feeders, they hunt at the bottom of their habitat
KIND: Ray-finned fish

While catfish are found just about everywhere, half of the thousands of species live in the Americas. Catfish don't have scales.

PARROTFISH
SPECIES: 100
LIVE IN: Mostly coral reefs
EAT: Sea plants and corals
KIND: Reef fish

Parrotfish have very unusual prominent and human-looking teeth, with which they gnaw vegetation. People in Southeast Asia find parrotfish very good to eat.

CRABS
SPECIES: 4,500
LIVE IN: All the world's oceans;
850 species live in rivers and lakes
EAT: Mainly algae, but almost anything
KIND: Decapod (ten-legged) crustacean

Crabs move mostly by walking sideways on eight of their limbs. The other two limbs are strong pincers for gripping. They may communicate with each other by drumming their pincers.

CUTTLEFISH
SPECIES: 120
LIVE IN: Eastern Atlantic Ocean,
and Asian and Australasian waters
EAT: Small shellfish, worms, and
other cuttlefish
KIND: Cephalopod mollusc

Cuttlefish, like squid, are cephalopods, which means they are closely related to octopuses, and like them, have tentacles.

SHARKS
SPECIES: 440
LIve IN: Most oceans, but
especially common off Australia,
and the western United States
EAT: Mostly smaller fish; some
prey on seals and sea lions

Sharks vary in length from the 8-inch (20-cm) dwarf lanternshark to the 40-foot (12-m) whale shark. But all are highly efficient predators.

BRISTLE WORMS
SPECIES: Close to 10,000
LIVE IN: Just about everywhere
EAT: Rotting flesh and algae

Bristle worms have bristles on their leg-like parapodia and are the most common of all marine organisms.

OTTERS
SPECIES: 13
LIVE IN: Shallow coastal and
river waters
EAT: Sea-dwelling otters eat urchins
and other shellfish
KIND: Mustelid (weasel-like) mammal

Sea otters live on the west coast of North America, and off Russia and Japan. Marine otters live in estuaries on the west coast of South America and are the world's smallest sea mammals.

SPECIAL SKILLS

As with the animals featured in this book, there are many that have a skill that's so special and so much more amazing than anything humans could do. Most ocean creatures have unusual features, but some are better or at least stranger than others.

TURTLE MAGNETS

Loggerhead sea turtles hatch from eggs on a beach. Then they swim far across the ocean for years, before returning to the same beach to lay their own eggs. They may travel more than 4,000 miles (6,400 km) away. So how do they find their way back? After all, the ocean has no landmarks and the turtles were just a day old when they set out.

Scientists have recently discovered that the turtles can sense Earth's magnetic field. It seems that each part of the coast has its own magnetic signature. The turtles remember this, and use it as a compass to navigate home.

MARVELOUS MIMICS

The mimic octopus is one clever sea creature. It's especially good at pretending to be other animals. By taking on their color and way of moving, it can appear to be anything from a lionfish to a cluster of sea snakes.

The tiny black marbled jawfish can imitate the movements and camouflage of a mimic octopus imitating a lionfish! That way it can hitch a ride on the octopus and use the octopus as its disguise while foraging for food!

STRANGE COMPANIONS

The pearlfish and the sea cucumber (left) have a very strange relationship. The pearlfish lives in the sea cucumber's bottom. The sea cucumber is an animal, despite its name—but it's not much more than a mobile gut. For the pearlfish, the cucumber's anus is very appealing.

Usually, the pearlfish backs in, leaving its head sticking out. If it can't get back in after it's been out hunting, it simply moves on to another cucumber. Sometimes, though, the pearlfish dives in headfirst and starts gnawing away at the cucumber's inside. Then the cucumber shoots out its gut along with the pearlfish, and grows another one.

ARMED ASSASSIN

The blue ocean slug's blue topside makes it very hard for seabirds to see from above. But it's also an underwater ninja. It has no fear of the Portuguese man-of-war's stinging tentacles. It attacks and eats them, including the stinging cells. Then it sends the stinging cells it has swallowed to the tips of its own appendages to create stinging weapons.

PULLING THE TRIGGER

Triggerfish got their name from a very strange secret. They are tough reef-living fish that can fight off many attackers. They also have a set of interlocking spines that lock up to stop predators and wedge themselves into hiding places. Fishermen in Polynesia discovered they could trigger the fish to unlock its spines very easily—simply by pressing on a small dorsal fin.

INDEX

THE AUTHOR

John Farndon is Royal Literary Fellow at Anglia Ruskin University in Cambridge, United Kingdom, and the author of a huge number of books for adults and children on science, technology and nature, including international best-sellers. He has been shortlisted four times for the Royal Society's Young People's Book Prize.

THE ILLUSTRATOR

Cristina Portolano was born in Naples, Italy, and studied in Bologna and Paris, graduating in Comics and Illustration. Her artwork has appeared in Italian magazines and comic books such as *Delebile* and *Teiera*. She lives and works in Bologna, and her first book has recently been published by Topipittori.

Picture Credits (abbreviations: t = top; b = bottom; c = center; l = left; r = right)
© www.shutterstock.com:

2 cl, 6 cl, 6 bl, 7 cl, 7 tr, 7 br, 9 bl, 11 tl, 12 br, 15 br, 17 tc, 19 tr, 21 bl, 22 br, 25 tl, 27 tr, 30 tl, 30 br, 31 tl, 31 bl, 32 cr.

31 cr Sylke Rohrlach